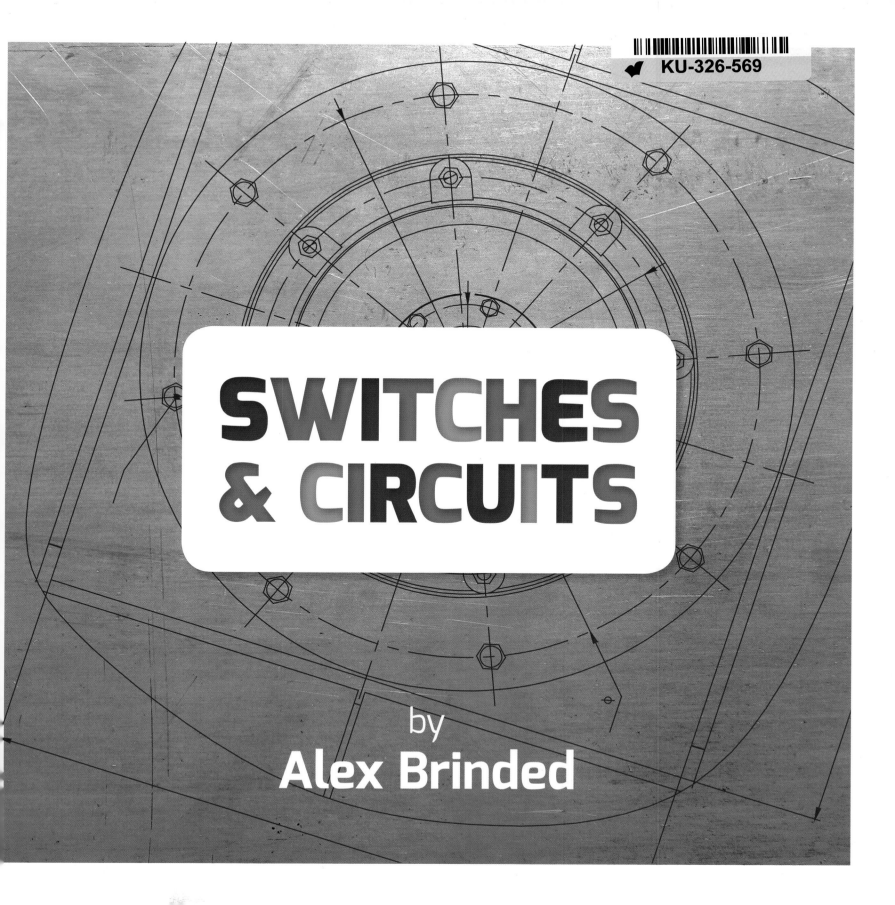

SWITCHES & CIRCUITS

by

Alex Brinded

©2018
Book Life
King's Lynn
Norfolk PE30 4LS

ISBN: 978-1-78637-306-9

All rights reserved
Printed in Malaysia

Written by:
Alex Brinded

Edited by:
John Wood

Designed by:
Gareth Liddington

A catalogue record for this book
is available from the British Library.

CONTENTS

Words that look like this can be found in the glossary on page 24.

WHAT IS ELECTRICITY?

Electricity is a type of energy. People have found many ways of making and using electricity, because it is very useful for lots of things.

Lightning is electricity that happens between the ground and clouds.

This is a nuclear **power station** which uses radioactive fuel.

Energy plants like this one make electricity by burning fuels, or using special **radioactive** fuel. Energy can also be generated using wind, water and sunshine.

HOW DO WE GET ELECTRICITY?

A Plug and a Socket

Lots of machines need electricity to work. Electricity flows along wires. When we plug a machine into a socket, the electricity goes through the wires and into the machine.

Mains electricity is the electricity that comes out of the socket. It is carried from power stations by big wires. The wires are made thinner and the electricity is delivered into buildings.

Pylons hold up the wires which carry electricity across large distances.

WHAT IS A CIRCUIT?

A circuit is a loop of wire that connects a **device** to a **power source**. Every electrical machine has a circuit. The circuit allows electricity to flow around the different parts of the machine.

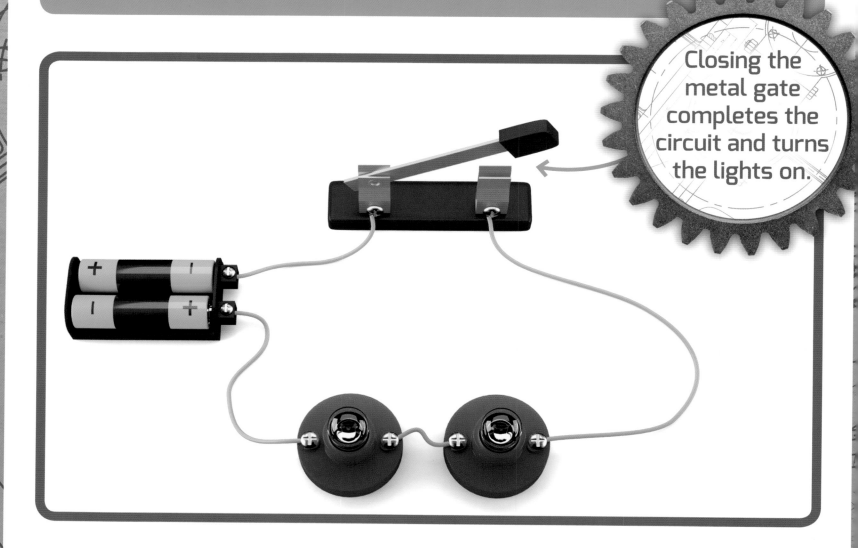

Closing the metal gate completes the circuit and turns the lights on.

This toy car uses electricity to make the wheels turn.

Mains electricity and batteries are power sources. Connecting a device to a power source using wires completes a circuit. When the device is turned on, electricity flows through the circuit, making the device work.

SWITCHES

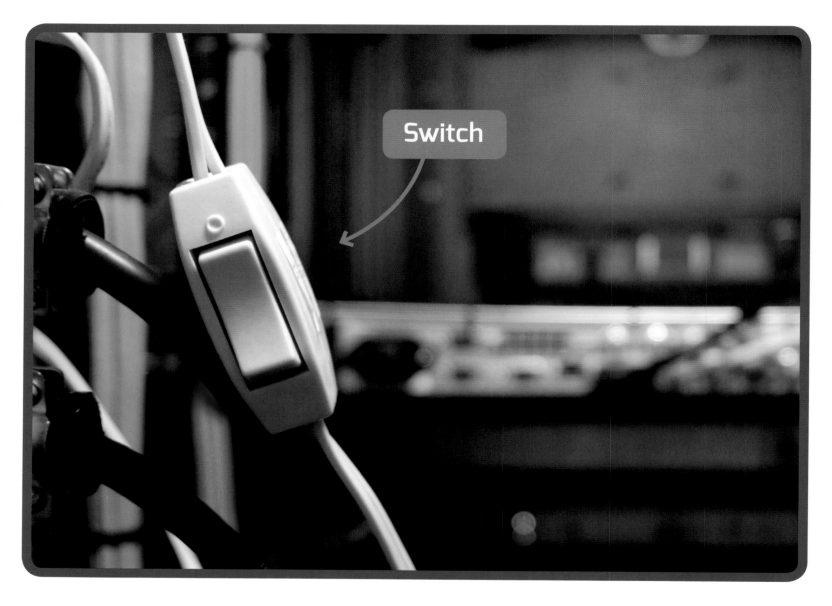

Switch

In order to turn machines on and off, the flow of electricity has to be stopped and started when we need it. This is what a switch does.

A switch controls the flow of electricity. It stops it by creating a gap in the circuit that electricity can't travel across. This is called breaking the circuit.

Turning the switch on completes the circuit.

BATTERIES

Batteries are power sources that store electricity. Some batteries need to be replaced after a while, and others need to be **charged**.

Battery

Batteries can power something anywhere – even in the sky!

This is a car battery, which powers the **motor** and engine in a car.

Electricity can be stored in batteries. Batteries allow some electrical devices to be used without being plugged in. We can take them with us and use them in different places.

WIRES

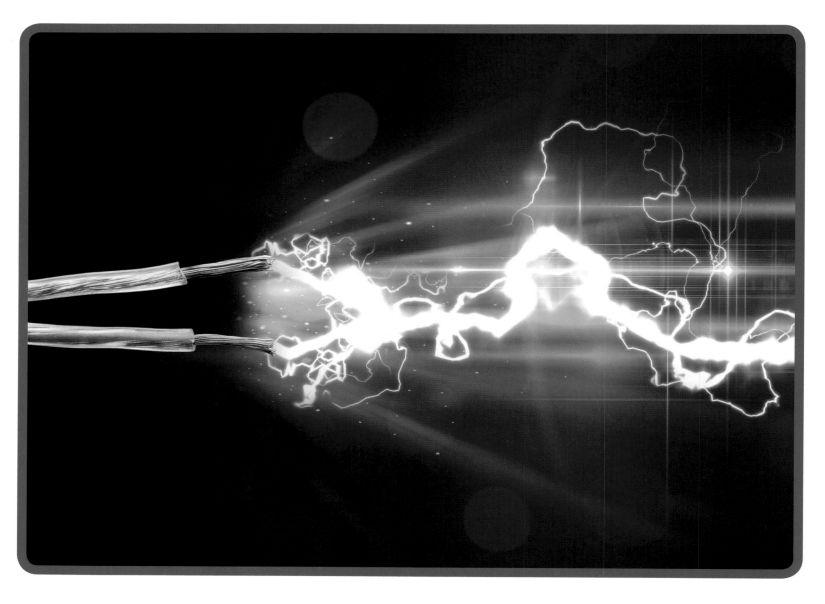

Devices, switches and batteries are all connected with wires. Wires used in circuits are made of metal because electricity travels through metal easily.

The wires in our homes are covered in plastic. Electricity doesn't travel through plastic very well, so it keeps us safe from an **electric shock**.

Wires

CIRCUIT BOARDS

A circuit board is a special metal board which extremely small devices are attached to. They **enable** machines to do different tasks, by using metal circuits to carry information.

Circuit Board

A circuit board in a mobile phone.

MOBILE PHONE

A circuit board in a mobile phone has to be small enough for the phone to be pocket-sized, whilst also helping it make calls, take pictures, send messages and use the Internet.

COMPUTERS AND LAPTOPS

How many devices can you think of which need to be plugged in?

Desktop computers are built to be used on top of desks and are powered by mains electricity. The screen and the computer are plugged in and switched on separately.

Laptops and tablets are types of computers that are made to be carried around. They use rechargeable batteries. A fully-charged laptop or tablet can be used anywhere.

Can you think of other devices that use a battery?

ELECTRICITY OVERHEAD

Trams are powered by overhead wires. A **pantograph** sticking out from the top of the tram remains in contact with a wire. Electricity flows through the wire, down the pantograph and to the motor, which turns the wheels.

Pantograph

Dodgems, or bumper cars often have large metal poles attached. The poles touch a metal grill on the roof. Electricity flows through this grill which powers the cars so they can be driven.

SWITCHING ON

Electric Vehicle Charging Station

Electric Bus

This electric bus is plugged into a charging station.

Electric vehicles don't use fuel. They have to be plugged into the mains electricity to charge their batteries before they can be driven.

Electricity has to be delivered to all these buildings and switched on in order for the lights to work. That's a lot of electricity!

Look how many lights are turned on!

GLOSSARY

charged	filled up with electricity
device	a machine that is made for one thing
enable	make something possible
electric shock	the shock someone receives when electricity goes through them
motor	a device that turns electricity into movement
pantograph	metal pole connecting a tram to an electric cable
power source	something that supplies power to a device
power station	places that make and send electricity
radioactive	a material which gives off radiation (a type of energy)

INDEX